FALL CRAFTS ACROSS CULTURES

12 Projects to Celebrate the Season

BY MEGAN BORGERT-SPANIOL

CAPSTONE PRESS
a capstone imprint

Dabble Lab is published by Capstone Press, an imprint of Capstone.
1710 Roe Crest Drive, North Mankato, Minnesota 56003
capstonepub.com

Library of Congress Cataloging-in-Publication Data
Names: Borgert-Spaniol, Megan, 1989– author.
Title: Fall crafts across cultures: 12 projects to celebrate the season /
by Megan Borgert-Spaniol.
Description: North Mankato, Minnesota: Capstone Press, [2023] | Series:
Seasonal crafts across cultures | Includes bibliographical references. |
Audience: Ages 8–11 | Audience: Grades 4–6 | Summary: "Fall is a season
of celebration! Join the fun with twelve festive crafts that celebrate
holidays from around the world. Create yarn apples for the Jewish
holiday Rosh Hashanah. Mix soothing slime to mark World Mental Health
Day. It's always the season for crafting!"— Provided by publisher.
Identifiers: LCCN 2021061501 (print) | LCCN 2021061502 (ebook) | ISBN
9781666334586 (hardcover) | ISBN 9781666334593 (pdf) | ISBN
9781666334616 (kindle edition)
Subjects: LCSH: Handicraft—Juvenile literature. | Autumn—Juvenile
literature.
Classification: LCC TT160 .B756 2023 (print) | LCC TT160 (ebook) | DDC
745.5—dc23/eng/20220121
LC record available at https://lccn.loc.gov/2021061501
LC ebook record available at https://lccn.loc.gov/2021061502

Image Credits
Project and materials photos: Mighty Media, Inc.

Design Elements
Shutterstock: KALYA MALYA, lukeruk, sherilhome

Editorial Credits
Editor: Jessica Rusick
Designer: Sarah DeYoung

All internet sites appearing in back matter were available and accurate when this
book was sent to press.

Printed and bound in the USA. PO4882

TABLE OF CONTENTS

Fall

What is your favorite part of fall? Is it the fresh school supplies or colorful leaves? Maybe it's all the seasonal celebrations, including Halloween, Rosh Hashanah, and Thanksgiving!

Celebrate fall with cool projects that reflect the season. Craft a floating light for Diwali or a citrus-stamped towel for Sukkot. You might even build a glowing sugar skull for Day of the Dead or a nature mosaic for Indigenous Peoples' Day. Fall is filled with enough natural beauty and festivities to keep you crafting all season long!

BASIC SUPPLIES

beads

cardboard

craft glue

crayons

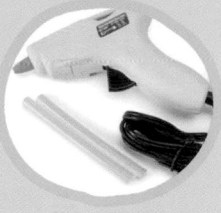
hot glue gun

yarn

paint and paintbrushes

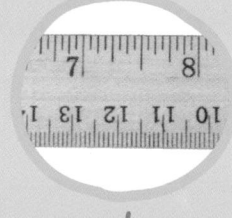
ruler

scissors

twine

CRAFTING TIPS

Be prepared! Read through the materials and instructions before starting a project. Cover your workspace with paper or plastic to protect it from messes or spills.

Think outside the book! Lots of the projects in this book use materials you'll likely find around your home. Is there something you can't find? Think of ways to adapt the project using items you do have.

Ask first! Get permission before using materials you find at home or school. Also ask before you collect items from nature and bring them indoors.

Be safe! Ask an adult for help with projects that require sharp or hot tools.

Clean up! When your project is complete, put all materials and tools back where you found them. Clean up any spills and wipe down your crafting surface.

To-Do List Dry-Erase Board

The start of a school year brings a fresh list of to-dos. Construct your own funky dry-erase board to hold task lists, reminders, or words of encouragement!

What You Need

- picture frame
- paint and paintbrush (optional)
- scissors
- craft tape
- dry-erase marker

What You Do

1. Take the cardboard backing out of the frame. If you want to paint the frame, carefully take the glass or plastic out of the frame too. Replace it when the paint is dry.

2. Cover the piece of paper or cardboard that comes in the frame with craft tape. Use light colors so the dry-erase marker will show on top of them.

3. Place the paper or cardboard back into the picture frame and secure the backing.

4. Use the dry-erase marker to write messages on the glass or plastic of the picture frame!

Fun Fact

School days are different in every country. In Finland, young students enjoy about 15 minutes of recess per hour!

SUKKOT

Citrus Stamp Tea Towel

A citrus fruit called the etrog is an important symbol during Sukkot, a Jewish festival of gratitude. But you can use any citrus fruit to make a homemade citrus stamp. Use it to refresh and brighten a plain old tea towel!

What You Need

- lemon, lime, or other citrus fruit
- sharp cutting knife
- small bowl
- paring knife
- paper towels
- fabric paint and paintbrush
- pie tin or small tray
- cotton tea towel

What You Do

1. Ask an adult to help you cut the citrus fruit in half. Save one of the halves for cooking or baking.

2. Gently squeeze the other citrus half over a bowl to remove some of the juice. It's okay if you don't get all the juice out. Refrigerate the juice for cooking or baking.

3. Ask an adult to help you carefully carve out the segments of flesh in your squeezed citrus half. Be sure to keep the walls between each section intact. Eat the cut-out sections or save them for later!

4. Use a paper towel to clean up any excess juice or pulp on the citrus half. Then let the citrus half dry out, cut end up, for about 15 minutes.

5. Spread a thin layer of fabric paint over the bottom of a pie tin or small tray. Dip the flat end of the citrus half in the paint. Make a few practice stamps on a paper towel.

6. Lay the tea towel flat on a protected surface. Use your citrus stamp to decorate the towel in any pattern you like.

7. Let the towel dry. Then display it where everyone can see!

ROSH HASHANAH
Yarn Apples

Rosh Hashanah is the Jewish New Year. It takes place in September or October. During this holiday, many people eat apples dipped in honey to symbolize hope for a sweet new year. Decorate your table with cute yarn apples in honor of Rosh Hashanah!

What You Need

- cardboard
- ruler
- scissors
- balls of red and/or green yarn
- twine
- green leaves (real or artificial)

What You Do

1. Cut a rectangle of cardboard that is 3 inches (7.5 centimeters) wide and 4 inches (10 cm) long.

2. Wrap the yarn around the width of the cardboard about 100 times, unraveling it from the ball as you go.

3. When you are done wrapping, cut the yarn off the ball. Carefully pull the wrapped yarn off the cardboard so it keeps its shape.

4. Cut a 10-inch (25.5-cm) piece of yarn. Slip the piece through the center of the wrapped yarn and knot to secure. This will create an apple shape. Don't cut off the extra tied yarn.

5. Cut a 10-inch (25.5-cm) piece of twine. Lay the twine across the knot you made in step 4. Secure the twine to the apple using the extra length of yarn.

6. Tie about eight knots into the twine to create the apple's stem.

7. Use the extra yarn to tie the leaf to the base of the stem. Then cut off any remaining bits of yarn and twine.

8. Repeat steps 2 to 7 to make more apples for your table!

NAVARATRI
Dandiya Sticks

Navaratri is a Hindu festival celebrating the triumph of good over evil. Many people celebrate Navaratri with a traditional dance called Dandiya. Dancers hold sticks that represent swords. Make your own Dandiya sticks out of newspaper and ribbons!

What You Need

- newspaper
- wooden skewer
- glue stick
- scissors
- ruler
- hot glue gun
- ribbon
- string
- beads
- buttons

What You Do

1. Lay a sheet of newspaper flat. Starting at one corner, begin to tightly roll the newspaper around a wooden skewer. Slide the skewer out once you've started the roll. Continue rolling. Spread glue onto the newspaper every few rolls until you reach the other corner. Glue the corner in place.

2. Lay another sheet of newspaper flat. Glue the middle of the roll you made to a corner of the new sheet. Roll the sheets together to build on the original roll. Glue the opposite corner in place.

3. Cut the ends of the newspaper roll so it is 14 inches (35.5 cm) long. This is your dandiya stick!

4. Hot glue the end of a ribbon to one end of your dandiya stick. Wrap the ribbon around the stick, gluing every few inches, until all the newspaper is covered.

5. Cut a 6-inch (15-cm) piece of string and tie a knot at one end. Thread beads onto the string.

6. Hot glue the unknotted end of the string to one end of your Dandiya stick. Use buttons and glue to cap both ends of the stick.

7. Repeat steps 1 to 6 to make a second Dandiya stick. Now you are ready to dance!

13

WORLD MENTAL HEALTH DAY

Soothing Foam Slime

World Mental Health Day takes place in October. Why not care for your own mental health with a few mindful minutes? This foam slime will help focus your senses and calm your mind.

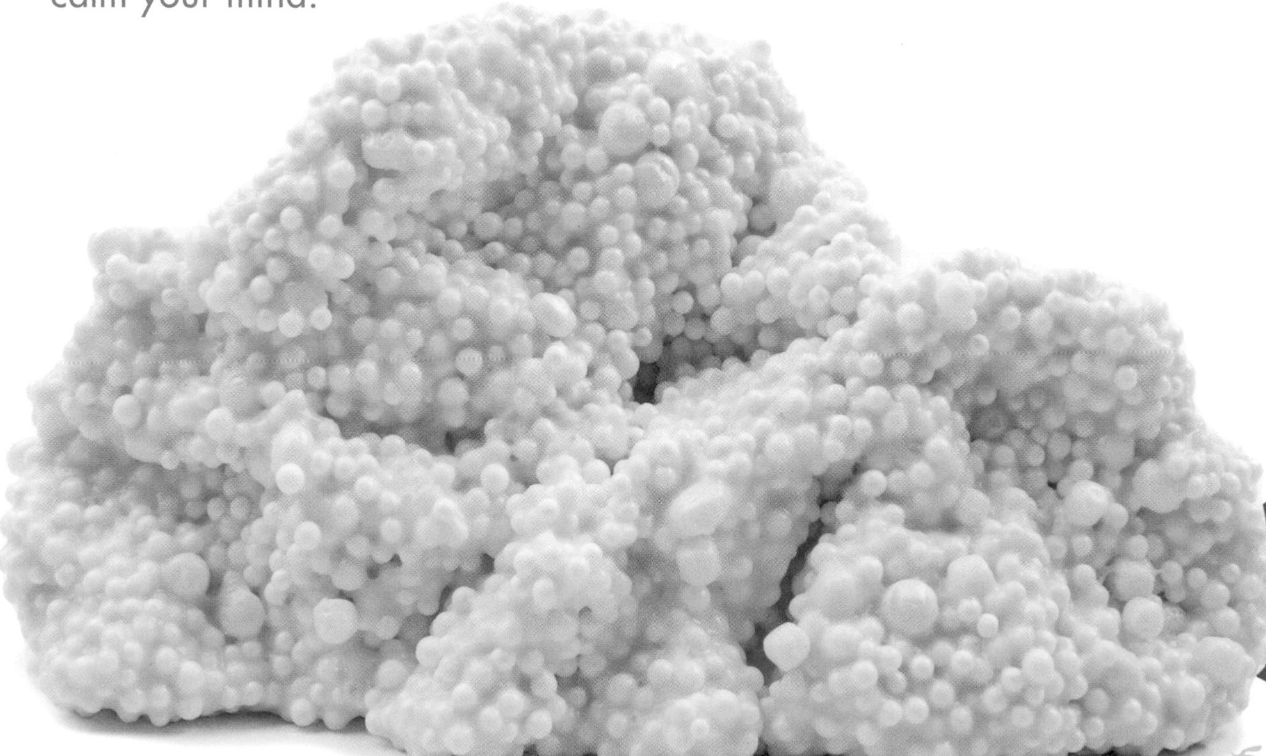

What You Need

- measuring cup and spoons
- borax
- water
- bowls
- craft stick for mixing
- craft glue
- food coloring
- foam beads

What You Do

1. Pour ½ teaspoon (2.5 milliliters) borax into 1 cup (0.24 liters) warm water. Stir until the borax dissolves. Set the solution aside.

2. In a large bowl, mix 1 cup (0.24 L) craft glue and 1 cup (0.24 L) water. Mix food coloring into the glue mixture until you've reached your desired color.

3. Add 3 tablespoons (44 mL) of the borax solution to the glue mixture. Mix in more solution a tablespoon at a time until you've created a mass of slime.

4. Pour 2 cups (0.47 L) of foam beads into a second large bowl. Add the slime to the second bowl and begin mixing in the beads.

5. Keep adding more foam beads, ½ cup (118 mL) at a time, until the slime cannot hold any more.

6. Play with your slime! Notice how it feels and sounds as you squeeze it. Wash your hands after handling the slime.

15

INDIGENOUS PEOPLES' DAY

Natural State Mosaic

Indigenous Peoples' Day honors Native Americans and their histories. As the first inhabitants of what is now the United States, Native people lived off the land around them. Gather bits of nature to make a mosaic of your home state. Then research the Native nations and tribes that first settled the land you live on.

What You Need

- cardboard
- scissors
- ruler
- paint (brown, white) and paintbrushes
- pencil
- collected bits of nature, such as twigs and dandelions
- hot glue gun
- twine
- pushpin
- brass fastener

What You Do

1. Cut a piece of cardboard 12.5 inches (32 cm) long and 10.5 inches (26.5 cm) wide.

2. Paint the cardboard. To make it look like whitewashed wood, paint a layer of brown and then white. Let the paint dry after each layer.

3. Sketch or trace an outline of your state on the cardboard.

4. Arrange collected bits of nature within the outline of your state. Glue down the bits of nature.

5. Cut a 12-inch (30.5-cm) piece of twine. Knot the ends together to make a loop.

6. Use the pushpin to make a hole near the top of your artwork.

7. Push the brass fastener through the hole. Slip the twine loop around the fastener legs. Flatten the legs against the cardboard. Your mosaic is ready to hang up!

17

SEASONAL CRAFT
Fall Fairy

Fall is a time of dramatic transformation in nature. Trees burst into fiery colors. Leaves fall and branches turn bare. Go on a fall walk to collect bits of nature. Then use these pieces to create a fairy in honor of the season!

What You Need

- collected bits of nature, such as acorns, twigs, and stones
- hot glue gun
- tweezers (optional)

What You Do

1. Select an item that could be the body of your fairy, such as a pine cone or piece of birch bark.

2. Select an item to be your fairy's head, such as an acorn or stone.

3. Glue the fairy's head to its body.

4. Glue twigs or winged seeds to the body for arms or wings.

5. Add any final embellishments, such as a flower petal hat, to your fairy. Use tweezers to help transfer flower buds and other small materials as needed.

6. Glue your finished fairy to a stone or bark base so it can stand on its own!

DAY OF THE DEAD
Glowing Skulls

Day of the Dead is a Mexican holiday celebrated in early November. According to tradition, the spirits of loved ones rejoin their families on this day. Many people celebrate by painting skulls on their faces or decorating their homes with sugar skulls. Make your own glowing skulls using plastic eggs and LEDs!

Fun Fact

In Spanish, Day of the Dead is known as Día de los Muertos.

What You Need

- black paint and paintbrush
- LED tea lights
- plastic eggs
- pushpin
- screwdriver
- pliers
- black permanent marker
- images of sugar skulls (optional)
- hot glue gun (optional)

What You Do

1. Paint the bases of the LED lights black. Let them dry.

2. Ask an adult to help you poke several holes in the top of a plastic egg using a pushpin. Have the adult use a screwdriver to expand the small holes into one big hole.

3. Have the adult use pliers to expand the hole even more. It should be large enough to fit the flame of an LED tea light.

4. Use a black permanent marker to draw a skull on the plastic egg. Add details like leaves, dots, hearts, and flowers. If you'd like, look up images of sugar skulls on the internet for inspiration.

5. Push an LED tea light's flame into the hole. If you'd like, hot glue the egg to the light base. Turn on the LED to make your skull glow.

6. Repeat steps 2 to 5 to make more glowing skulls!

Crayon-Drip Pumpkin

Thanksgiving is a harvest celebration that dates back to colonial America. Historians say pumpkin was on the table at the first Thanksgiving meal in Plymouth, Massachusetts. Pumpkins remain a popular symbol of the fall harvest. Today, many Thanksgiving feasts include pumpkin pie!

Fun Fact

Potatoes of all kinds are another popular Thanksgiving dish. But historians say this root vegetable would not have been on the menu at the first Thanksgiving.

What You Need

- crayons
- craft knife
- hot glue gun
- white pumpkin
- newspaper
- hair dryer

What You Do

1. Pick out crayon colors to paint your pumpkin with. Peel the paper off the crayons. Break each crayon into pieces about ½ inch (1.3 cm) to 1.5 inches (4 cm) long. Use long pieces for a large pumpkin and short pieces for a small pumpkin.

2. Have an adult help you cut the crayon pieces in half the long way with a craft knife. This helps the crayons melt faster.

3. Hot glue the crayon pieces around the pumpkin stem, flat sides down.

4. Place the pumpkin on a large surface covered in newspaper.

5. Hold a hair dryer about 3 inches (7.5 cm) above the crayons to melt them. On the hair dryer's highest setting, this will take about 5 minutes. It will take longer if the crayon pieces are long or thick.

6. Let the crayon wax dry. Then put your pumpkin on display!

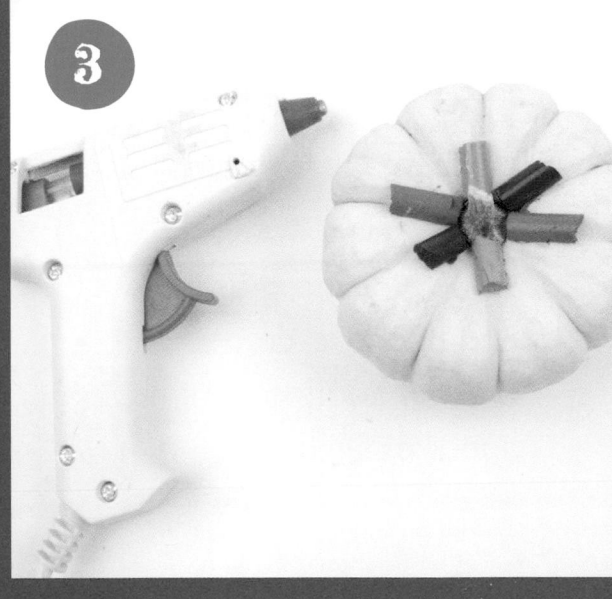

DIWALI
Floating Light

Diwali is often called the Festival of Lights. It's a time for gathering and exchanging gifts with loved ones. During the five-day celebration, clay lamps fill homes and temples with light. You can use a glass jar and beads to create a colorful floating light in honor of Diwali!

Fun Fact

Diwali is a major holiday in India, where most of the population is Hindu. But it's celebrated across the world by people who practice Hinduism, Jainism, or Sikhism.

What You Need

- glass jar with lid
- hammer and nail
- paint and paintbrush (optional)
- craft wire
- ruler
- wire cutter
- pliers
- hot glue gun and/or craft glue and paintbrush
- beads
- tweezers (optional)
- LED tea light

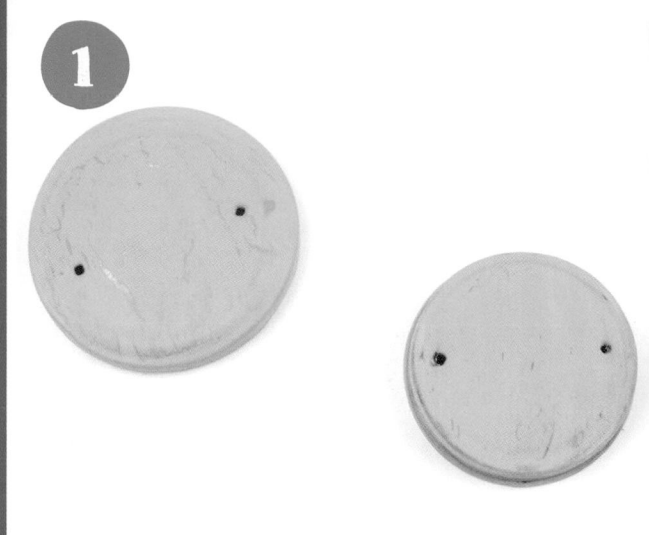

What You Do

1. Have an adult poke two holes in the lid of a jar, one near each edge, using a hammer and nail. If you'd like, paint the lid a color of your choice. Let the paint dry.

2. Cut an 8-inch (20-cm) piece of craft wire. Put each end of the wire into a hole in the lid to form a handle. Use pliers to tightly loop the wire ends on the underside of the lid.

3. Cover the surface of the jar with beads. If you are using tiny beads, paint regular craft glue onto the jar and roll the jar over the beads. If you are using large beads, attach them to the jar with hot glue and tweezers.

4. Place an LED tea light in the jar and secure the lid. Then hang your floating light up!

Pine Cone Wreath

Putting up a wreath is a simple way to celebrate any season. Give your door a golden autumn glow with this wreath made of painted pine cones!

Fun Fact

A pine cone's purpose is to house seeds. Its scales stay closed to keep the seeds safe from cold or damp weather. When the weather turns warm and dry, the scales open to spread the seeds!

What You Need

- about 50 pine cones of various sizes
- paint (red, orange, yellow) and paintbrushes
- craft glue
- floral foam wreath (10 to 12 inches, or 25.5 to 30.5 cm)
- newspaper
- ruler
- scissors
- twine
- hot glue gun

What You Do

1. Paint the tips of the pine cone scales red, orange, and yellow. Let them dry.

2. Spread craft glue over the floral foam wreath. Wrap the foam in newspaper. This creates a bulkier surface to glue the pine cones to.

3. Cut a 24-inch (61-cm) piece of twine. Knot the ends of the twine together to form a big loop. Wrap the twine loop around the wreath to make a hanger.

4. Glue the pine cones to the wreath. Start with the largest pine cones. Then fill in the gaps with smaller pine cones until your wreath looks full.

5. Hang your wreath up using the twine loop!

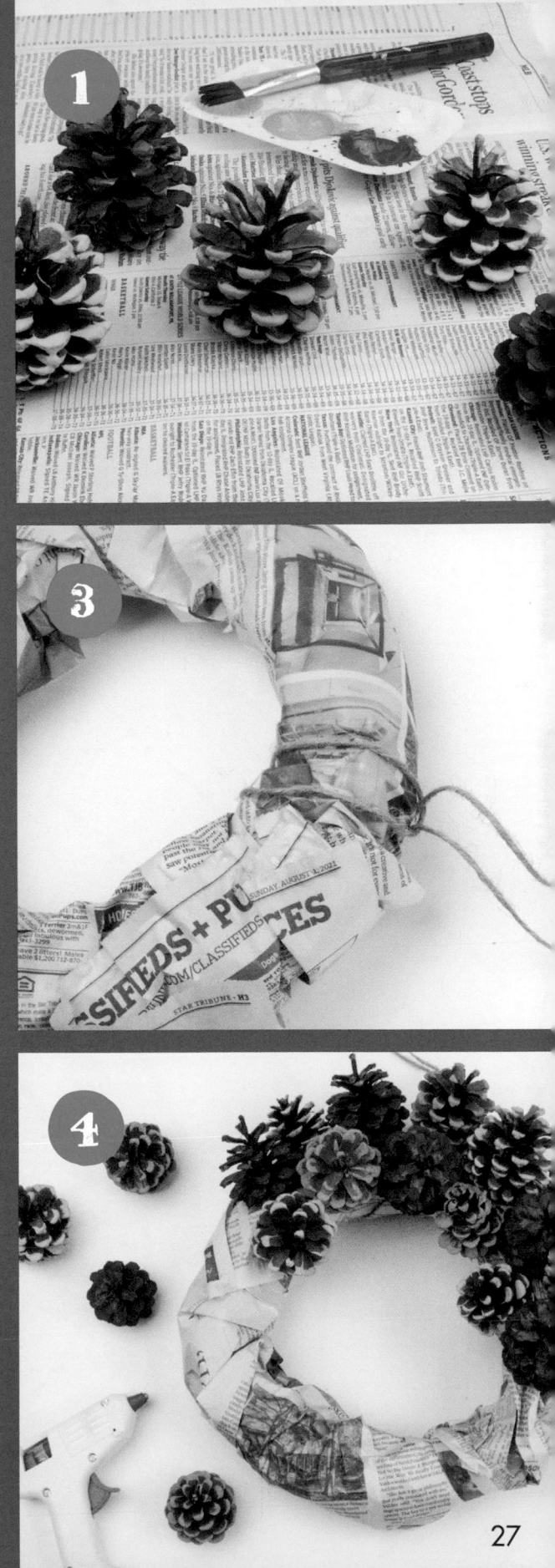

Sticky Spiderweb

Halloween dates back to an ancient Celtic festival where people wore costumes to hide from ghosts. Dressing up in costume is still a popular Halloween tradition. So is putting up spooky decorations, like this creepy spiderweb!

What You Need

- medium bowl
- craft glue
- water
- measuring cup and spoon
- paint (optional)
- mixing spoon
- yarn
- ruler
- scissors
- tape
- wax paper
- chenille stems
- beads
- hot glue gun
- fishing line

What You Do

1. Mix ¼ cup (59 mL) craft glue and 1 tablespoon (15 mL) water in a medium bowl. If you want a colored web, mix in a few drops of paint too.

2. Cut four 16-inch (40.5-cm) pieces of yarn and six 30-inch (76-cm) pieces of yarn.

3. Tape together two sheets of wax paper and lay them on your work surface. Make sure the wax paper surface is big enough to fit one 16-inch (40.5-cm) yarn piece vertically and horizontally.

4. Dip the four 16-inch (40.5-cm) pieces of yarn into the glue mixture so they are completely covered.

5. Pull each yarn piece out, lightly pulling them between two fingers to remove excess glue.

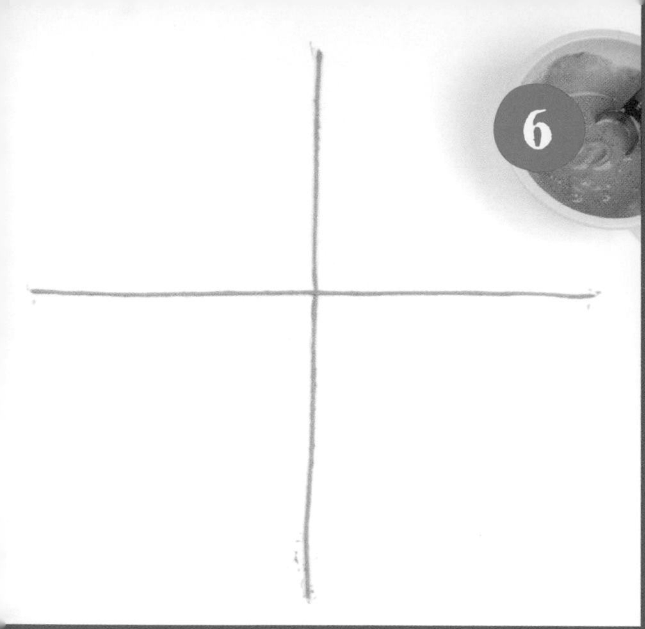

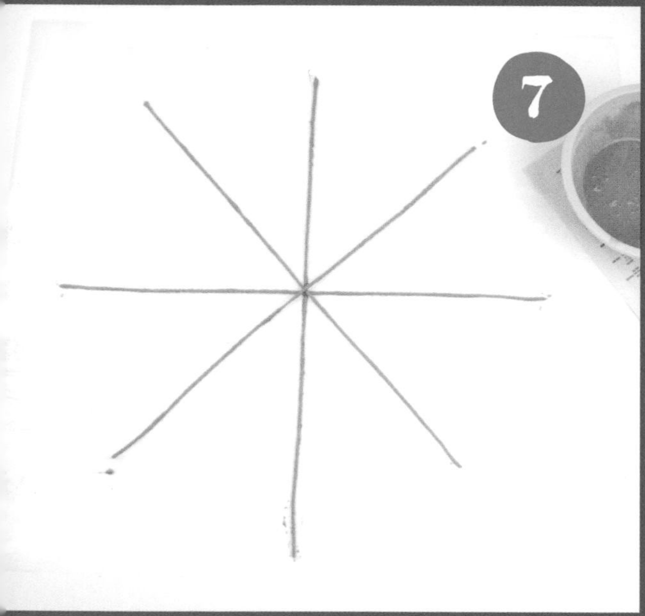

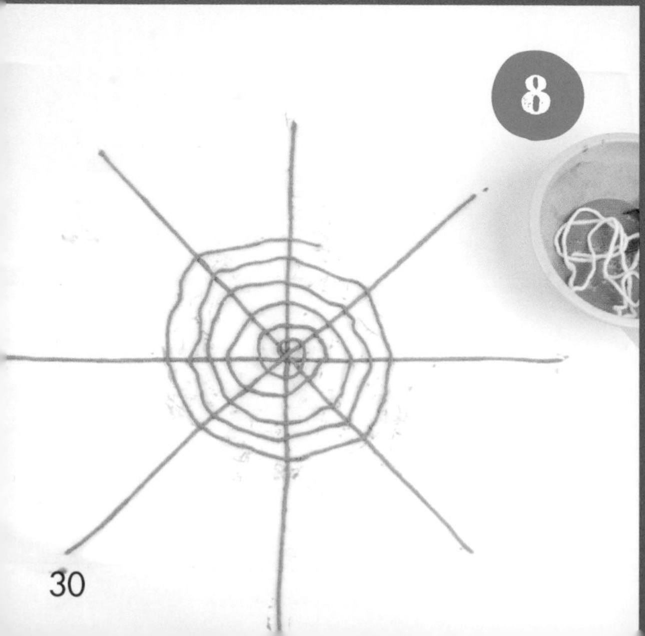

6. Place two glue-covered pieces of yarn in the shape of a plus sign onto the wax paper.

7. Place the other two glue-covered yarn pieces in the shape of an X over the first shape.

8. Repeat steps 4 and 5 with a 30-inch (76-cm) piece of yarn. Starting at the center of your web shape, lay the yarn over the web so it spirals out toward the open ends. When you reach the end of a yarn piece, cover the next piece with glue and start where the previous piece left off. Once the web is complete, let it dry for up to 24 hours.

9. While the web dries, make your spider. Group together four chenille stems and bend them all at their centers. Twist them below the bend to form the head of the spider.

10. Separate the eight stem ends into two groups of four. These are your spider's legs.

11. Thread two beads onto each leg. Bend the leg at each bead.

12. Once the web is dry, carefully remove it from the wax paper. Use hot glue to reconnect any portions that came apart.

13. Use fishing line to hang up the web. Then place your spider in the center!

READ MORE

Borgert-Spaniol, Megan. *Super Simple Halloween Activities: Fun and Easy Holiday Projects for Kids*. Minneapolis: Abdo Publishing, 2018.

Stewart, Whitney. *What Do You Celebrate? Holidays and Festivals around the World*. New York: Sterling Children's Books, 2019.

Thompson, Heidi E., and Marcy Morin. *Create with Cardboard*. North Mankato, MN: Capstone Press, 2021.

INTERNET SITES

35 Fun Back-to-School Crafts to Show Off Your Personality
goodhousekeeping.com/home/craft-ideas/g22593259/back-to-school-diy

What Are the Five Days of Diwali?
wonderopolis.org/wonder/What-Are-the-Five-Days-of-Diwali

What Is Indigenous Peoples' Day?
dosomething.org/us/articles/indigenous-peoples-day

ABOUT THE AUTHOR

Megan Borgert-Spaniol is an author and editor of children's media. When she isn't writing or reading, she enjoys doing yoga, eating croissants, and crafting homemade pizzas. Megan lives in Minneapolis, Minnesota, with a tall, goofy man and a small, chatty cat.